FRESH-PICKED POETRY

A Day at the Farmers' Market

Michelle Schaub

Illustrated by
Amy Huntington

Charlesbridge

To Maci, Ethan, and Ben: my favorite farmers' market treasure hunters—M. S.

For Pat: garlic farmer extraordinaire—A. H.

Published by Charlesbridge
85 Main Street
Watertown, MA 02472
(617) 926-0329
www.charlesbridge.com

Library of Congress Cataloging-in-Publication Data
Names: Schaub, Michelle, author. | Huntington, Amy, illustrator.
Title: Fresh-picked poetry: a day at the farmers' market / Michelle Schaub;
    illustrated by Amy Huntington.
Description: Watertown, MA: Charlesbridge, 2017.
Identifiers: LCCN 2016013777 (print) | LCCN 2016020751 (ebook) |
    ISBN 9781580895477 (reinforced for library use) |
    ISBN 9781632895738 (ebook) | ISBN 9781632895745 (ebook pdf)
Subjects: LCSH: Farmers' markets–Juvenile poetry.
Classification: LCC PS3619.C334 F74 2017 (print) | LCC PS3619.C334 (ebook) |
    DDC 811/.6–dc23
LC record available at https://lccn.loc.gov/2016013777

Printed in China
(hc) 10 9 8 7 6 5 4 3 2 1

Illustrations done in watercolor, water-soluble graphite, ink, and Photoshop
Display type set in Catalina Avalon Slab Bold by Kimmy Design
Text type set in Tonic-Bold by T-26
Color separations by Colourscan Print Co Pte Ltd, Singapore
Printed by 1010 Printing International Limited in Huizhou, Guangdong, China
Production supervision by Brian G. Walker
Designed by Susan Mallory Sherman

Market Day Today

It's market day.
Hooray, hooray!
Spy the wonders
on display:

    rainbow carrots,

        herb bouquets,

        heaps of berries,

            sample trays.

Farmers chat.
Musicians play.

    A neighbor–

    stroller–

        dog parade.

Join the party;
don't delay!
Come celebrate;
it's market day!

Early Risers

While you sleep,
snuggled tight,
farmers toil
by silver light.
Harvest, sort,
wash, and load.
Hop in trucks.
Hit the road.
Just as dawn
pinks the sky,
they arrive,
stretch, and sigh.
Set up tables,
tents, and bins.
By the time
your day begins,
the farmers' day
is in full swing—
enjoy the bounty
that they bring.

Transformed

Parking lots once jammed with cars,
busy city blocks,

school yards near the monkey bars,
boardwalks by the docks,

quiet small-town neighborhoods,
bustling railroad stations,

now teem with farmers and their goods—
tasty transformations.

Pile Up

Farmer Rick's meticulous
when setting up his stand.
He places all his items
into stacks precisely planned.
His cauliflower towers
take him eons to align.
His pyramids of peppers
show impeccable design.
Not one sloppy heap of beets,
no single misplaced pea.
Each veggie castle he constructs
has perfect symmetry.
But when Miss Mallory arrives,
Rick sports a wary smile—
she always picks her produce from
the *bottom* of the pile!

Is It Ripe?

Can you stare at some cherries
      and find a hint there?
Does the squeeze of a peach
      help you compare?
Will the smell of a melon
      give clues you can use?
Can a tap on an apricot
      help you to choose?
How do you pick fruit
      that's ripened just right?

      Just ask the farmer—
            she'll give you a bite.

TRY ME!

SAMPLES

Delightful Bites

Alluring aromas float over tent tops—a whiff of vanilla, a whisper of spice.

A hint of some cinnamon dusted on cupcakes, a sniff of plump blackberries tucked into pies.

CINNAMON ROLLS

cupcakes

Follow your nose to the freshly baked loaves: oatmeal, sourdough, whole wheat, and rye. Croissants and muffins, still warm from the oven, so tempting, so scrumptious. Which ones will you try?

BENNE wafers

Baklava

Tamales

MUFFINS

Bread

Necessary Mess

It clings to boots
and radish roots
and smudges mushroom caps.

It likes to hide
tucked deep inside
all crannies, grooves, and gaps.

In tater skins
and onion bins,
the farmer's fingernails.

POTATOES

GREEN BEANS

Potted Herbs & Flowers

rAdiSheS

In curly greens,
on stringy beans,
old crates, and weighing scales.

This film of dust,
a thin brown crust—
a mess you can't avert.

But don't you know?
No crops would grow
without a lot of dirt.

Market Melody

*Twing, twang, twiddle,
thrum-a-rum–*
fiddles pluck
and banjos strum.
*Rink, dink, rattle-
skattle* band,
jammin' near
the jelly stand.
*Fee, fi, faddle,
skiddley-skee–*
catch the market
melody!

Sally's Sweet Corn

Sally's Sweet Corn

Get your roasted sweet corn here!

Can't be beat this time of year!

Eat it fast.

Eat it slow.

Crunch in circles.

Nibble rows.

Wipe the butter off your chin.

Ear to ear, you're sure to grin.

Quick, before it disappears!

Step right up–

the sweet corn's here!

Summer Checklist

If . . .

- ✓ the pavement is so hot it could roast a shish kebab,
- ✓ the temperature is high enough to pop corn off its cob,
- ✓ boatloads of tomatoes and zucchini reach the sky,
- ✓ the watermelon vendor slices fruit for all to try,
- ✓ a line wraps round the corner for fresh-squeezed lemonade,
- ✓ dalmatians and their owners are both panting in the shade,
- ✓ farmers mist the Swiss chard and themselves to feel revived,

then . . .

without a doubt, you can shout: "Summer has arrived!"

Goose Chase

We're on a chase,
a wild-goose chase,
a wild gooseberry chase.

Down the rows,
around each stand,
we're searching everyplace.

We'll buy a pint;
we'll buy a quart;
we'll buy them by the case.

To make some jam
and bake a pie
with crust of lattice lace.

They won't last long;
they'll soon be gone;
that's why we need to race.

We're on a chase,
a wild-goose chase,
a wild gooseberry chase.

Antonio's Old-Time Sharpening

Can you find the grinder?

Listen for the *grrr*.

A *grrrowly grrroan*

as steel meets stone,

and wheels spin in a *blurrr*.

He'll sharpen rusty sheers and clippers,

as the old gears *purrr*.

Dull knives will beam,

and scissors gleam.

Dizzzy, whizzzy whirrr.

From Bee to Me

Fields of clover with roaming bees,
nectar collected busily.
Hives abuzz with activity,
combs enclosing sweet mystery.
Keepers' smoke calms the jamboree,
jars of liquid-gold alchemy.
City,
market,
and (finally)
me.

Face Painting

Local Loot

Pirates dig for riches
on distant island shores.
Bargain hunters rummage
through shelves of old thrift stores.
Divers search for gems and gold
on ancient sunken ships.

We find and *eat* our treasures
on local market trips.

Wild Dreams in Two Voices

GREEN ZEBRA TOMATO	**DINOSAUR KALE**

If I were a real zebra . . .

And if I were a dinosaur . . .

my stripes would reach from tail to mane.

I'd have sharp teeth and roar.

I'd graze upon the grassy plain.

I'd rule the jungle scene.

You'd be extinct—it's sad but true.

Your stripes would not be green.

But I'd be fast.

And I'd be fierce.

We'd both be wild and strong.

But you would hunt,

and you'd be prey.

We wouldn't get along.

I guess we should be thankful.

Let's accept our fate.

As fruit

and leaf,

we live in peace—
upon a salad plate.

Farmer Greg's Free-Range Eggs

Shaded brown,
soft green, or beige,
they range
in shape and size.
But nestled well
in speckled shells,
there hides a rich surprise.
All laid by hens,
not cooped in pens,
but roaming free and bold,
these eggs are
eggs-traordinary,
with yolks
as pure as gold.

Clues in Blue

Blue splatters on our T-shirts.
Blue speckles on our shoes.
Blue splotches on our baskets.
Our footprints? They're blue, too.

Blue juice upon our fingers.
Blue lips, blue tongues, blue smiles.
Blue prints on empty cartons
once brimming with blue piles.

"Who gobbled up the berries?"
We both were reprimanded.
We tried to hide the evidence—
but we were caught . . .

BLUE-handed.

Day's End

The musician's notes have hushed.
The grinder's stone is still.
No more eager customers
with shopping bags to fill.
The produce crates are empty.
Good-bye to honey jars.
The line of tents has vanished,
replaced by rows of cars.
Home cupboards brim with bounty,
while families dream away,
imagining the wonders
     to come
        next market day.

Fresh-Picked Reasons to Spend a Day at the Market

From Alabama to Alaska, there are more than eight thousand farmers' markets in the United States, double the number there were a decade ago. Why should you go?

Tempt Your Taste Buds: You'll find the crispiest, juiciest, most flavorful foods at the farmers' market. Grocery-store produce is usually picked before it's ripe and stored for days or even weeks. Market fruits and veggies, on the other hand, are harvested and sold at the height of ripeness. Fresh-picked treasures travel straight from the farm to your fingertips.

Go Wild on Variety: Green zebra tomatoes. Dinosaur kale. Dragon's tongue beans. You'll discover plenty of rare wonders at the farmers' market. Instead of growing one crop for mass production, small-scale farmers plant a variety of items. Many farmers use heirloom seeds, which have been passed down from generation to generation and produce delicious, colorful, and unique crops. Sink your teeth into heirloom fruits and vegetables, and you're in for a taste adventure.

Use Fewer Resources: Food at the grocery store travels an average of 1,500 miles to get to your plate. That's the distance from California to Kansas! Farmers' market goods usually trek less than two hundred miles to be sold. Just think of the gas you help save when you buy local! You'll save even more if you walk or ride your bike to your local market day.

Befriend a Farmer: Get to know the people who harvest your honey and pick your peas. The vendors at farmers' markets love to chat with customers and answer questions. You can learn about where food comes from and know that you're supporting local family farms and businesses.

Learn More: To find your local farmers' market, visit **www.localharvest.org** and type in your zip code. Or you can download the FarmLine app to a tablet or smartphone. Be sure to tell your friends and neighbors about your market, too!